Seize Opportunity It's YOUR Season!

by
Debra B. Morton

Seize Opportunity
It's YOUR Season!
ISBN 0-9657706-1-3
Copyright © 2005 by
Debra B. Morton
9661 Lake Forest Blvd.
New Orleans, La 70127

Published by
Phos Publishing, Inc.
Tulsa, Oklahoma

Text Design: Lisa Simpson

Contents

Acknowledgments

This has been a very busy year for me, and I could not have accomplished the things I did without the help of great people around me. I give special thanks to my wonderful husband for always being the wind beneath my wings. You have given me many opportunities to gain experience through serving. Serving you has taught me the importance of timing and to *seize opportunity*. Thanks, Honey.

To my loving children: Jasmine, Paul Jr., and Christiann. You have made many sacrifices with both parents being in ministry. You have always been very encouraging – supporting my ministry and everything I do. Lord, thanks for another breath of freshness, Gigi's baby, E. J. Ross.

I am very grateful to my mother, father, and siblings for allowing me to be me.

Heartfelt thanks to Linda Dugas-Drummer, my executive assistant, for proficiently and willingly performing balancing acts with my multifaceted lifestyle.

Les, our meeting was providential – nobody but God! Thanks for your unselfishness and the rich deposit you poured into my life. I look forward to our many great years ahead.

Hats off to D. B. Morton Ministry Team.

Accolades to my church family for all the love, prayers, and support you have continuously shown to me from early childhood to becoming your co-pastor.

Love to my most recent blessed opportunity – Changing a Generation Full Gospel Baptist Church – of which I am the proud senior pastor. In a little time you have already afforded me an opportunity that I will always praise God for, and the best is yet to come.

Most importantly, God ever inspires me to write and pursue dreams and visions, and I am grateful to be used as a vessel to deliver this message.

Foreword

These are times unlike any we have ever experienced before. Fear and uncertainty about the future are permeating the air. Bankruptcies, home foreclosures, and job losses are at an all-time high.

In the midst of the conflict in the Middle East and global turbulence, many people are searching for answers that could lead them out of this **wilderness experience** to the **land of promise of a better life.**

Seize Opportunity, a creatively written and inspired book by **Debra Morton,** provides a road map that will empower you to carve a tunnel of hope through the mountains of despair. Drawing from her years of pastoring, travel, and dynamic leadership in the **Greater St. Stephen's Ministries, Debra** gives us practical, tried and proven methods based on **God's Word** that will provide you new insights and views of prominent biblical figures and examples that will inspire you to pursue your dreams with passion and determination.

This "no excuse is acceptable for failing" approach, teaches you the step-by-step process to live a healthy, happy, and prosperous life. **Debra** reminds us to **"seek ye first the kingdom of God,"** and through the application of **His Word,** all things that your heart desires will be **added unto you.**

Each page of this book is designed to connect you with your God-given personal power that will enable you to exercise **authority and dominion** over every area of your life.

It has been said, **"Opportunity does not knock – it stands by silently waiting for you to recognize it."** This book, written with clarity and simplicity, will help you see your life with new eyes and *Seize Opportunity!*

Les Brown, Speaker and Author
Live Your Dream
It's Not Over 'Til You Win
Up Thoughts for Down Times
<u>www.lesbrown.com</u>

Introduction

I am so excited about this season. It is the season of grace and opportunity. Number five represents grace, so this year – 2005 – marks the beginning of this season of grace. Grace is present in abundance for those who love God – to experience the success of God.

Grace – the unmerited favor of God – is now present for you to seize opportunity. Opportunity will begin to manifest in areas never experienced or expected. Opportunity will come, no doubt, but will you be ready to seize it? Will you be strong enough, brave enough, humble and obedient enough to receive it and give God the glory?

The Bible says we are destroyed for a lack of knowledge or information (Hosea 4:6). Is that necessary? No! God has prophetically sent His Word and instructions so we will not be destroyed but so we will be victorious in all of our endeavors.

Opportunity can make or break you. Better still, you can make or break opportunity. This book, *Seize Opportunity,* will make you aware of yourself as well as your surroundings, and it will cause you to improve on both of them. Your success and opportunity will not come without challenge, but the tools and qualities you will gain in this season will prepare you and have you ready when opportunity knocks at your door.

I am excited about your future in God. Grace is upon you. David slew his Goliath and you will slay yours too. It's your season! Be blessed!

Debra B. Morton

These are the words of the Holy
One, the True One, He Who has the
key of David, Who opens and no one
shall shut, Who shuts and no one shall
open:

I know your [record of] works and
what you are doing. See! I have set
before you a door wide open which
no one is able to shut; I know that you
have but little power, and yet you have
kept My Word and guarded My
message and have not renounced or
denied My name.

Revelation 3:7-8 AMP

Chapter 1

Recognizing Opportunity

And the Philistine said, I defy the armies of Israel this day; give me a man, that we may fight together.

When Saul and all Israel heard those words of the Philistine, they were dismayed, and greatly afraid.

Now David was the son of that Ephrathite of Bethlehem-judah, whose name was Jesse; and he had eight sons: and the man went among men for an old man in the days of Saul.

And the three eldest sons of Jesse went and followed Saul to the battle: and the names of his three sons that went to the battle were Eliab the firstborn, and next unto him Abinadab, and the third Shammah.

And David was the youngest: and the three eldest followed Saul.

But David went and returned from Saul to feed his father's sheep at Bethlehem.

And the Philistine drew near morning and evening, and presented himself forty days.

And Jesse said unto David his son, Take now for thy brethren an ephah of this parched corn, and these ten loaves, and run to the camp to thy brethren;

And carry these ten cheeses unto the captain of their thousand, and look how thy brethren fare, and take their pledge.

Now Saul, and they, and all the men of Israel, were in the valley of Elah, fighting with the Philistines.

And David rose up early in the morning, and left the sheep with a keeper, and took, and went, as Jesse had commanded him; and he came to the trench, as the host was going forth to the fight, and shouted for the battle.

For Israel and the Philistines had put the battle in array, army against army.

And David left his carriage in the hand of the keeper of the carriage, and ran into the army, and came and saluted his brethren.

And as he talked with them, behold, there came up the champion, the Philistine of Gath, Goliath by name, out of the armies of the Philistines, and spake according to the same words: and David heard them.

And all the men of Israel, when they saw the man, fled from him, and were sore afraid.

And the men of Israel said, Have ye seen this man that is come up? surely to defy Israel is he come up: and it shall be, that the man who killeth him, the king will enrich him with great riches, and will give him his daughter, and make his father's house free in Israel.

And David spake to the men that stood by him, saying, What shall be done to the man that killeth this Philistine, and taketh away the reproach from Israel? for who is this uncircumcised Philistine, that he should defy the armies of the living God?

1 Samuel 17:10-26

Opportunity Is a Blessing

Toward the end of the year 2004 I was watching CNN as they were doing interviews about famous people. They were highlighting things that had happened in their lives in 2004. As I was watching the interview with P. Diddy, the reporter asked,

15

"How are you doing all that you do? I mean, you have an empire when it comes to music. Now you are on a political path and you have a fashion empire. How do you do it?"

P. Diddy replied, "Well, I feel that I have been blessed with opportunity so I must take advantage of it. I have to focus because I've been given all these things and I must give back."

As I listened to the exchange, God spoke to me. He said, "Did you hear that?" P. Diddy said that he was blessed with opportunity. This is why the Scripture says the world is wiser than we are. P. Diddy realized that opportunity was a blessing from God. Then God said to me, "Many times My people do not realize that *opportunity is a blessing*. Not everyone is blessed with opportunity and not everyone gets the same opportunity."

Opportunity
is a blessing.

How many times have you either said or heard others say, "Oh, if I had that opportunity. If only I had that chance." The Lord reminded me that we often forget that when opportunity comes, we need to recognize first that it is a blessing and secondly we must learn how to take advantage of it.

I believe strongly that we are in the season of grace in the year 2005. I believe that the unmerited favor of God is all around us and upon us, so opportunity will seem to "come out of the woodwork." Opportunity is coming your way, but you must seize it for yourself.

> We are in the the season of grace
> in the year 2005.

Tuned In!

It is important to learn to recognize opportunity when it comes your way. King David, a mighty man of valor, one after God's own heart, recognized opportunity early on in his life. He is our example of one who seizes opportunity. He was asked to go to the battlefield to take food for his brothers, yet when he got there, he recognized opportunity.

How many times do we miss opportunity in our everyday tasks? We tend to think that our everyday job or our everyday existence is no big deal. Most people settle into their meager existence. They tend to feel pitiful, down, depressed, and even hopeless as they get further behind in their finances, suffer with physical ailments, and/or battle with difficult relationships.

God is addressing this issue with His people in this hour. He longs for us to be attentive and listen closely to His voice, learning daily from His Word so we will recognize each God opportunity in the midst of our day-to-day routines.

"**Early** [in the morning] **will I seek thee . . .**" (Psalm 63:1). When we rise each morning, we should tune in to God and look for His blessings. We should anticipate the touch of His hand that pushes us forward and listen for His voice that says, "Go! It's your season!"

David's Opportunity

David's opportunity began with a simple request. His father asked him to go to the battlefield where three of his older brothers were stationed. Jesse had no E-mail and news filtered in slowly from the front lines. So he asked David to take food to his brothers as well as to the officers in charge. In return, Jesse simply wanted news of his sons' welfare.

This was a lesser task, not a big deal, but David could have whined and asked his father to send a servant. We are not told in Scripture what David was feeling at the time. Perhaps he was excited about the opportunity to see something other than sheep. Perhaps he was excited because he missed his brothers. David could have thought, *Here I go again running around for someone else's benefit. Again, I am nothing but an errand boy doing unimportant tasks.*

We are unaware of David's feelings or mind-set until he gets there. All we see is David's obedience. "**David rose up early in the morning, and left the sheep with a keeper, and took, and went, as Jesse had commanded him; and he came to the trench, as the host was going forth to the fight, and shouted for the battle**" (1 Samuel 17:20).

Obedience in the small things is critical. The Apostle Peter admonishes us, **"Humble yourselves therefore under the mighty hand of God, that he may exalt you in due time"** (1 Peter 5:6). In the parable of the talents Jesus said, **"His lord said unto him, Well done, thou good and faithful servant: thou hast been faithful over a few things, I will make thee ruler over many things . . ."** (Matthew 25:21).

> "Thou hast been faithful over a few things,
> I will make thee ruler over many things . . ."
> (Matthew 25:21).

Opportunity Found in Serving

We may feel that something is unimportant, but all God is asking is for us to be obedient. Often we can miss great opportunity because we refuse to be submissive – to be a servant. Often we miss opportunity because it's on a shelf in the servant's quarters. Opportunity is often found in serving. While you are helping someone else or doing some simple, mediocre task, it may be an opportunity from God that will catapult you into your destiny.

Listen and Obey

The key with David is, *he obeyed his father.* We must obey our Father at His first command. I am convinced that now, more than ever before, we must listen carefully for the still small voice of God in our every decision. Our footsteps are ordered by God (Psalm 37:23). When we hear Him, we must heed His voice.

> "Likewise, ye younger, submit yourselves unto the elder. Yea, all of you be subject one to another, and be clothed with humility: for God resisteth the proud, and giveth grace to the humble" (1 Peter 5:5).

People are being gunned down in fast-food restaurants and killed in mall parking lots while shopping. These are routine, everyday life situations, so it is important to have God's input in each step we take. Today people can be taken out at work by a disgruntled former employee, but if we listen for the Father's voice and obey, He will warn us and protect us.

> Our footsteps are ordered by the Lord (Psalm 37:23).

I am amazed at the stories of people who were spared from some tragic event because "something" told them not to go or "something" just didn't feel right. We must obey the Father's voice at a moment's notice. When we hesitate to question God on the matter or delay our actions trying to figure out why we feel something different, we may miss a God-given opportunity.

When David arrived at the battlefield, he took care of his responsibilities as it related to the food his father had sent, but he began to hear strange rumblings from the battlefield. David heard the giant talking. The Bible tells us that other men had fled because they were afraid. However, David did not flee. Instead, he had questions: "What is going on? Who is this uncircumcised Philistine?" In his spirit, he was hearing something more than the rumblings of a crazy man. He heard opportunity.

Developing a "Different Ear"

When you recognize opportunity, you will hear what other people do not hear. You will respond differently to that which is going on. When others are quitting, hiding, or running, you will continue on because you have a different ear.

I believe we must develop a "different ear" to hear opportunity's knock. David had been anointed to be king as a young boy. He knew his destiny. Yet he continued to fine-tune his ears to hear the voice of God for direction. Just because God has shown or spoken destiny concerning you, you cannot ignore His voice of direction to get there.

> We must develop a
> "different ear" to
> hear opportunity's knock.

21

I believe David developed his hearing in the wilderness while tending the sheep. Most of us don't like being in the field. We don't want that wilderness experience. We don't like that "alone" time. Many would rather do anything else than spend time "shut in" with God. But we need that time alone with the Lord. God pushed us there, for it's beneficial to us to seize and maintain opportunity.

In your alone time you gain confidence and increase your faith in God. You discover that if Mother isn't there or if Daddy isn't there, even if there are no friends around, God is still with you.

> "I will never leave thee,
> nor forsake thee"
> (Hebrews 13:5).

We need to learn how to pray alone. Many people cannot pray when the crowd is around because there is no intimate relationship with God.

> "The grace of the Lord Jesus Christ,
> and the love of God,
> and the communion of the Holy Ghost,
> be with you all. Amen"
> (2 Corinthians 13:14).

Psalm 1:2 says, **"In his law doth he meditate day and night."** As you develop an ear for God's voice and learn His Word, you will begin to hear things that others do not hear, because you have been still enough and alone enough to know His voice.

Once you have fine-tuned your hearing, you will be able to recognize the voice of God above all other voices. When others are all around you and everyone is talking, you will hear something greater.

> "My sheep hear my
> voice, and I know them,
> and they follow me"
> (John 10:27).

Evaluating Opportunity

Another aspect of recognizing opportunity is being able to evaluate each opportunity. This does not mean that you question God, but you realize all opportunity is not God opportunity. Opportunities pass by us daily, but we must learn to discern what is good and what is evil (Hebrews 5:14). We must be certain that each opportunity we encounter is a God-given one.

Be careful not to seize a moment because a moment is just what you get. You may seize a moment to run after money, a perm, a position, or people. It could be your emotions or your financial situation controlling you.

> "He that is spiritual
> judgeth all things . . ."
> (1 Corinthians 2:15).

When people are in a bind, they will grab at almost anything that feels good or looks good. But friend, investigate the opportunity. Make certain that it is God, because if it is not God, you may get things in a moment, but all you will have is momentary stuff. Momentary pleasure. Momentary peace. Momentary success. Momentary prosperity. Only a moment.

Sometimes when you take a momentary opportunity, the real thing will come shortly thereafter, but you will have cut yourself off from your genuine God-given opportunity.

For example, sisters, you may have gotten caught up with Harold and then God's real opportunity comes passing by in Jonathan. You see Jonathan, but Harold has your attention and your emotions all locked up.

Brothers, you may be caught up with Barbara, but along comes Mary. You should have waited for your God-given opportunity instead of being "caught up" in the moment.

Sometimes you simply get caught up in being comfortable. You used to want to move on, but you got comfortable and now you don't think you have the strength you need to move on.

24

A moment becomes a lifetime. As a child of God, you cannot get settled in a moment. You must listen and wait for your God-given opportunity.

> "But they that wait upon the Lord
> shall renew their strength; they shall mount up
> with wings as eagles; they shall run,
> and not be weary; and they shall walk,
> and not faint"
> (Isaiah 40:31).

How do you recognize or know for sure when your God-opportunity comes? Well, when it is God, you will be motivated by God to do it. When you have spent your alone time with God and you have learned to recognize His voice, you will know by your spirit, not by your mind or by mere emotions.

David recognized a God opportunity. Again, he heard something different. Obviously, he heard God calling him. Sometimes you may be overwhelmed by the opportunity. You may feel that you simply are not qualified. If life has taught me anything, I have learned that God does not always call the qualified, but He always qualifies the called!

> God does not always call the qualified,
> but He always qualifies the called!

You may recognize the voice and the hand of God, but feel you are not the one for the opportunity. You aren't sure how you even got there. You don't even know why your supervisor chose you. True, you may not possess all the techniques you need, but God will work it out.

If God calls you to do something, He will qualify you. If you don't know how you got the call, don't fret about it. You got it because it was your God-given opportunity.

Secondly, when you are presented with such an opportunity, it will fit into the plan of God for your life. David heard what he heard because God gave him an opportunity to showcase his skills as a warrior. It was God's plan for him later to become the captain of the army. Later in life as David performed as captain of the army, it ignited the people in praise of David, setting the stage for him to become the king of Israel.

The door was opened by Saul to place David over the army. However, it was really God's opportunity to set in place the house of David, out of which would come the Lord Jesus Christ Himself.

> "For promotion cometh neither from the east,
> nor from the west, nor from the south.
> For God is the judge: he putteth down one,
> and setteth up another"
> (Psalm 75:6-7).

When you recognize that God might be up to something in your life, check it out. Does it agree with the teachings of the Word of God? For example, Brother so-and-so is not your husband opportunity if there is already a sister so-and-so. Money cometh is not your God-given opportunity if you have to lie, steal, manipulate, or take it from someone else.

If you have a God-given opportunity to get a new car, it is not going to ruin your budget or cause you to miss payments on other bills you already have.

When you evaluate an opportunity, judge it by the Word. Count up the cost and then pray until God's peace comes. The enemy is a liar. The truth is not in him (John 8:44). He will present counterfeit opportunities. His opportunities can put you in debt, in the hospital, in jail, or give you hell on earth. Again, when opportunity comes, evaluate. Contemplate the Word. Meditate on God's truth and ask for His peace.

> "And let the peace of God rule in your hearts . . ."
> (Colossians 3:15).

Intimate Fellowship with God

David had such an intimate relationship with God that when his opportunity was presented, he seized it. He grabbed hold and did not have a moment of doubt in spite of the naysayers. David had to seize the opportunity while it was within his reach. You can't seize it when it's gone.

What I love about David's journey is that it was simply one of obedience. He was going about the business of serving his father.

> "We will obey the voice
> of the Lord our God, to whom we send thee;
> that it may be well with us,
> when we obey the voice of the Lord our God"
> (Jeremiah 42:6).

When we are about the Father's business, His opportunities will come. David's ears perked up when he heard a strange voice threatening the army of God. The giant declared that he was going to destroy the army of God and the Israelites were cowering in fear. David knew at that moment it was time to stand up for God.

Fear is not of God. When it's time to seize your opportunity, you will boldly stand against fear. David knew this was it. His opportunity was at hand and it was time to grasp it. Although David knew that he had an anointing for kingship (1 Samuel 16:1-17), he also knew he could not force it to happen.

> "To every thing there is a season, and a time to every purpose under the heaven" (Ecclesiastes 3:1).

You can't force your time. David understood that God had opened the door and everything that he had experienced in his life had led him to that place — the battleground. This was David's God-given opportunity!

Goliath: David's Door to Destiny

No one else that day could or would have stood against the raging giant. Amazing, Goliath was David's opportunity. He was the door to David's destiny and no one understood that more than the shepherd boy. It could not have been clearer to David that this was his time. His very presence on that battlefield signaled Goliath's doom.

David said, "It is time!" What do you do when you recognize your time? Number one, *you must be informed*. You must know what you are getting into, and more importantly, you must know who is with you. David asked, **"Who is this uncircumcised Philistine, that he should defy the armies of the living God?"** (1 Samuel 17:26). The people told him that it was Goliath and that he was going to kill them and eat them.

The day of opportunity requires us to be informed. Hosea 4:6 says, **"My people are destroyed for**

29

lack of knowledge. . . ." David asked the question for information.

There was some good news just in case someone could slay the giant. King Saul would give him his daughter's hand in marriage, full tax exemption, and great wealth, yet this information didn't move David. David was not moved by the good news or by the bad news. He was on assignment. He was not asking questions to get opinions or ideas. He just wanted the lowdown.

Number two, *he was not going to be influenced by what people thought or by worldly treasures of men.* He asked the question again, **"What shall be done to the man that killeth this Philistine, and taketh away the reproach from Israel? for who is this uncircumcised Philistine, that he should defy the armies of the living God?"** (1 Samuel 17:26). David was not questioning from a heart of greed, but from righteous indignation that anyone would dare to threaten God's people.

What man had to offer did not influence David. He simply refused to stand by while the army of God was being defied. David was influenced for the cause of righteousness. You cannot allow people and things that titillate your flesh to influence your decision to act. Your decision must be God inspired.

> "Through God we shall do valiantly:
> for he it is that shall tread down our enemies"
> (Psalm 60:12).

Opposition

Before David had done little more than investigate the situation, opposition came. No great surprise! Whenever you are facing a God-given opportunity, there will be opposition. Just because nothing is too hard for God (Jeremiah 32:17) does not mean that things you do for Him will be easy for you in your natural man.

David's first opposition came from within his own family. Does that sound familiar? David's three eldest brothers were part of Saul's army and they resented the boy. They, along with the other brothers, had been rejected by Samuel previously when Samuel sought a son of Jesse to anoint as king.

Eliab, David's oldest brother, heard David speaking with the other men on the battlefield and he was angry. Eliab asked David why he had left his few sheep. He accused David of being conceited and of having a wicked heart. Sadly, Eliab did not know David's heart but God did. David was a man after God's own heart (Acts 13:22).

> "Jealousy is cruel as the grave . . ."
> (Song of Solomon 8:6).

On the contrary, David had not become bored with watching sheep, for God was in the desert with David and He enjoyed a rich fellowship with him there. David's journey to the front lines was simply one of obedience.

David Was Focused

David did not respond to his brother's tirade. You see, in the desert David had learned to focus, so despite the annoying criticism, his focus was on the challenge that Goliath had made against the people of God.

David was persistent in his questions and because of it, Saul got word of the bold young man and sent for him. Saul must have been fascinated by the kid who had more self-confidence than the entire army camped there. David felt no need to build himself in Saul's eyes. He admitted that he was only a shepherd with a couple of victories under his belt – the lion and the bear. But now there was a big guy defying the army of the living God and so David withstood Saul's interrogation.

And David said unto Saul, Thy servant kept his father's sheep, and there came a lion, and a bear, and took a lamb out of the flock:

And I went out after him, and smote him, and delivered it out of his mouth: and when he arose against me, I caught him by his beard, and smote him, and slew him.

Thy servant slew both the lion and the bear: and this uncircumcised Philistine

shall be as one of them, seeing he hath defied the armies of the living God.

David said moreover, The Lord that delivered me out of the paw of the lion, and out of the paw of the bear, he will deliver me out of the hand of this Philistine. And Saul said unto David, Go, and the Lord be with thee.

1 Samuel 17:34-37

Perhaps sensing the hand of God on the young man, Saul gave David his blessing. In the process, however, he gave the kid his own tunic and armor and placed a bronze helmet on David's head. What a sight that must have been!

David could not even walk around, because he was not used to the heavy equipment. He gave up on Saul's uniform. It was simply another obstacle. God equips us for each opportunity. He shows us what to use and what to refuse.

However, David needed a weapon so he took his staff and from a stream nearby he chose five smooth stones. Then there was the opponent – David's opportunity – Goliath. The giant was nine feet tall and he was wearing a helmet and armor made of bronze weighing 125 pounds. The spear he carried weighed 15 pounds more. Goliath despised the boy who stood in front of him. He made fun of David and his pitiful weapon.

> "Who hath saved us, and called us with an holy calling,
> not according to our works,
> but according to his own purpose and grace,
> which was given us in Christ Jesus
> before the world began"
> (2 Timothy 1:9).

David's Time Had Come

While waiting for this opportunity, David had faced his lion and his bear in the field. He walked in obedience to his earthly father, Jesse, and he had constant fellowship with his heavenly Father. He faced jealousy, criticism, doubt, second-hand, ill-fitting battle wear, and taunting, but his time had come.

As God presented me with an opportunity — Women of Excellence fifteen years ago – I innocently said, "I am just going to do whatever God says to do," and fifteen years later I am still leading it. In spite of obstacles, I have held on. Each year or season of Women of Excellence I have continued to do what God has said to do. I am determined, and like it or not, I am going with God.

> "Now our Lord Jesus Christ himself,
> and God, even our Father, which hath loved us,
> and hath given us everlasting consolation
> and good hope through grace, comfort your hearts,
> and stablish you in every good word and work"
> (2 Thessalonians 2:16-17).

David refused to follow Saul's directions and wear his armor. It is important to remember that we cannot always follow people. People can mean well, be really sincere, but be sincerely wrong. David was obedient to Saul's leadership when he tried on the armor, but once he put it on, he realized that it would not fit. The Word says that it wasn't "tested" or "proven." David respectfully declined, saying that he would just use his own stuff.

And Saul armed David with his armour, and he put an helmet of brass upon his head; also he armed him with a coat of mail.

And David girded his sword upon his armour, and he assayed to go; for he had not proved it. And David said unto Saul, I cannot go with these; for I have not proved them. And David put them off him.

1 Samuel 17:38-39

People sometimes want to make you use their stuff. It is because they realize the anointing of God is on your life, so they insist that you use their stuff. Then, when God uses you they can get some of the glory. David knew he had to use only what God had given him so God alone could get the glory! It may not have looked like much to Saul, but in the hand of God, little becomes much.

Seize Opportunity
with Boldness and Confidence

David could go forth in confidence. He walked up to Goliath with five smooth stones and said, **"This day will the Lord deliver thee into mine hand; and I will smite thee, and take thine head from thee; and I will give the carcases of the host of the Philistines this day unto the fowls of the air, and to the wild beasts of the earth; that all the earth may know that there is a God in Israel"** (1 Samuel 17:46). David spoke in faith and with confidence.

> "For we walk by faith, not by sight"
> (2 Corinthians 5:7).

You may be facing some difficult things, but you have to seize opportunity. Things may seem insurmountable and unattainable, but if God says "Here's opportunity," take His grace and run with it. Sometimes you may have to cry, you may face challenges, but still seize the opportunity. God is with you.

David took that opportunity and became captain of the army. Eventually he became the king of Israel. But before he reached the throne, he was cursed, threatened, criticized, and misunderstood, but God had a plan.

David never feared Goliath the giant because he trusted God, the Greater One.

"They that trust in the Lord shall be as mount Zion,
which cannot be removed,
but abideth for ever"
(Psalm 125:1).

Search me, O God, and know my heart: try me, and know my thoughts: and see if there be any wicked way in me, and lead me in the way everlasting.

Psalm 139:23-24

Chapter 2

Self-Improvement

Each opportunity we are given is designed to bring us closer to our purpose or our destiny, the ultimate goal being, whatever we accomplish brings glory to God. You may have heard that opportunity can make or break you, but I say you can make or break opportunity.

We must use the grace of God in this season of opportunity to work on ourselves from the inside out as well as from the outside in. What appears on the outside reflects what's on the inside. If we are not whole on the inside, then opportunity can become a curse rather than a blessing. Whatever is within you is going to eventually come out of you. **"Out of the abundance of the heart the mouth speaketh"** (Matthew 12:34).

> "For the Lord seeth not as man seeth;
> for man looketh on the outward appearance,
> but the Lord looketh on the heart"
> (1 Samuel 16:7).

It is not about how great you look on the outside. It's about what's on the inside of you that tells the whole story. For example, if you are a poor manager of money, you will mess up with twenty dollars or with a hundred thousand dollars. Oftentimes we hear of someone who wins a big sum of money, but within a few weeks or a few months they are just as broke as they were before they won.

If you are a whoremonger, you could be a janitor or the President of the United States, it will come out. We must use God's grace and opportunity to improve from the inside out.

Check Your Motives

We must conquer the weaknesses of the inner man because when opportunity presents itself, ungodly motives will be exposed. We all want opportunity, but why? What's your motive? Opportunity is good, but why do you want it? Is it so that you can give God the glory, or is it because you want to jump ahead of others or fix somebody? Is it simply for selfish gain? It may be your love of money.

Whatever the reason, you must examine your motives. God-given opportunities are also for Him to get the glory. Are your motives pure, or do you want opportunity from God to show people how awesome you are?

> "And God is able to make all grace
> abound toward you; that ye,
> always having all sufficiency in all things,
> may abound to every good work"
> (2 Corinthians 9:8).

Shine or Serve?

God is not looking for those who want to shine. He is looking for those who want to serve. Not for stars, but servants. Do you find that there are opportunities all around you, yet you are over-looked? Perhaps God has already examined your motives.

> "But he giveth more grace. Wherefore he saith,
> God resisteth the proud,
> but giveth grace unto the humble"
> (James 4:6).

When David arrived at the battlefield, he was simply there in obedience. He was not seeking "his" moment. He was not looking for fame. He was not there chasing after opportunity, yet "bam." There it was! When God has something for you to do, when it's your season He will find you, even if you are in the servants' quarters.

David was in the field, working and taking care of the sheep. The prophet came to his house and brought the oil and asked Jesse to bring in all of his sons. He called in all of David's fine big brothers – the important ones, the ones with degrees, the handsome ones, those who thought they were great and wonderful – but Samuel the prophet was not satisfied.

He asked Jesse if there were any more sons. Jesse then thought of his son who was out in the field tending the sheep. Jesse sent for David. It was then that Samuel anointed David as king.

It does not matter if or where you are serving. God's opportunities will find you.

> "The hand of the diligent shall bear rule:
> but the slothful shall be under tribute"
> (Proverbs 12:24).

When David got to the battlefield he was already anointed to be the next king of Israel. David had a pure heart. People were talking about what Saul would give the man who would slay Goliath. David was not impressed or moved. He was not looking for power or material things in return for his service to the Lord's army. His eyes were on the enemy of Israel and of God.

David had a servant's heart. You must have the heart of a servant to please God. In fact, only those who give God glory in their personal victories or elevation are servants.

Showing Appreciation

Showing appreciation is another important quality to develop in seeking to improve your inner man. In difficult times we go to God in prayer. We may pray for a better job or a promotion or elevation, but we forget our prayers of praise. Remember to practice praise.

Sometimes we get so caught up in the things of life that when God's opportunities or blessings come, we take them too lightly. For everything good that comes our way, we should be grateful. Some of us need to get up off our blessed assurance and praise God!

> "Let us come before his presence with thanksgiving, and make a joyful noise unto him with psalms" (Psalm 95:2).

We have worried, planned, studied, prayed, and tried to figure it all out. We have spent hours on the problem, but sometimes we fail to spend a few minutes to give God the glory.

From the outside looking in, some have seen your struggles and some even wondered with you, *How could it ever work out?* But give God the glory. Show and tell them about the great and mighty God you serve.

I notice some of us in the Kingdom hate to be called a servant. You cannot stand it. You feel that servanthood is a thing of the past. History only. But Jesus said the servant is the greatest in the Kingdom.

True servanthood is an attitude and an attitude can be adjusted. Work on it. Improve your attitude and thank God. He is looking to bless and bestow opportunities on His servants.

> "Create in me a clean heart, O God; and renew a right spirit within me" (Psalm 51:10).

I can just hear David say, **"I had rather be a doorkeeper in the house of my God, than to dwell in the tents of wickedness"** (Psalm 84:10).

Investigate your motives and remain a servant on your way up to greatness. David remained a servant even though he was on his way up to becoming the king.

There are advantages to being a servant. Before you get to your elevated place, become a servant and you will feel what a servant feels. You will become sensitive to people who are now where you used to be.

Intoxicated with Arrogance?

Some of us become so intoxicated in our blessed place. As we get older we lord over people and treat them badly. In doing so, we miss opportunities to give God the glory. When people see someone with power and position operating as a servant, they see Jesus. They recognize that the person has the heart of Jesus, for Jesus operated in humility.

So even when mistreated, a servant of God responds like Christ: **"Father, forgive them; for they know not what they do . . ."** (Luke 23:34).

David was such a servant. He served his father Jesse, King Saul, his brothers, and sheep, so to run and take food to his brothers was not beneath him.

A person with a servant's heart will serve in whatever capacity is needed. They will stuff envelopes. They will empty the garbage. They will walk into the home of someone who is sick, hurting, or grieving and pick up a broom, wash the dishes, and fold the laundry. Nothing is beneath them if it will help the situation.

Rooted in Servanthood

Servants remember their roots and do not despise them. They remember where they came from and they are not ashamed. In fact, their past grounds them and develops such an attitude of gratitude that they become rooted in servanthood.

Jesus is our highest example of servanthood. He came to earth directly from the throne room of

47

heaven where He was seated at the right hand of God Himself. Paul said He [Jesus] **"being in the form of God, thought it not robbery to be equal with God"** (Philippians 2:6). Jesus thought nothing of coming to earth as a servant. It was His Father's request.

Jesus is our highest example of servanthood.

On earth Jesus reached out to the needy, the lowly, and the hurting. He rebuked the so-called hierarchy of the church for their high and mighty attitudes. He spoke with those of ill repute. He ate dinner with sinners. He developed a friendship with the despised tax collector. He admired the little people like the widow who gave all she had (Mark 12:42-44).

Jesus never took advantage of His position. He said, **"He that is least among you all, the same shall be great"** (Luke 9:48). The biography about the life of Mohammad Ali is titled, *The Greatest.* If you want to be great in the Kingdom of God, consider becoming the least.

When we do advance because of God's opportunity, we cannot abandon our ways of servanthood. We must never get so high and holy that we cannot serve. God knows your heart. You have no secrets from Him. Are you a servant?

> We must never get so high and holy that
> we cannot serve.

When your motives are right, you will be very clear on what God sends you to do. It will not matter where you are sent – to the White House or to the big house! You will understand your purpose there.

David was not interested in personal acclaim. He wanted to destroy the one who was coming against God's children. David was not seeking glory. He was serving God and all the glory would go to God.

Anytime you are in a circumstance where God is not being glorified, it is your assignment to step up to the plate. It is time for you to interrupt, respond like Jesus, and bring God's glory into the situation.

> Anytime you are in a circumstance where God
> is not being glorified, it is your assignment
> to step up to the plate.

When God puts you in the world and elevates you to a high place, it is not meant so that you can act all high and mighty. That is the way of the world. You are placed there to represent God – not yourself – and He alone should receive the glory.

Seeking God's Favor

Another area of self-improvement comes in the area of developing yourself to seek God's favor. We spend thousands of hours and millions of dollars during our lifetime seeking the favor of man. We want to look right. We want the proper degree by our name. We want to be thought of as intelligent. We want to read the right books. We want to have the best shape, the greatest hair, and the nicest clothes. All in all we want to be noticed and recognized for our achievements.

We all may be guilty of idolatry in that our greatest idol has become ourselves. We want the favor of man. In this year of grace, I believe the Church, the Bride of Christ, must begin to focus on gaining the favor of her Bridegroom, the Lord Jesus Christ. He would be the only One whose favor matters.

Check yourself. Do you want to improve for Christ's sake? Do you really desire to have the favor of God? Begin to take notice how many times each day you seek to impress someone. Write down for one day all that you have done to curry the favor of man. For most of us, this will be a reality check.

We may say we go to the gym to work out because it is good for our health and our heart, but is that really our motive? We may think we buy the clothes we do because we want to look presentable in the workplace or at church. Do we really? How much money and how much time do we spend at the hairdresser, in front of a mirror, admiring the view? I am not saying it is wrong to take care of the temple

God gave us. It is fine to make the most of what God has already given us, but who are we trying to impress?

It is a tough question, but we need to settle it. Do we seek the favor of God as often as we seek the favor of man? Get real. We need to check ourselves and then make some changes. Choose to improve. There is nothing wrong with knowing who we are, but we must be more aware of whose we are.

> There is nothing wrong with knowing who you are, but you must be more aware of whose you are!

The Word tells us that Jesus increased in favor with God and man (Luke 2:52). If you develop in the area of favor with God, the favor of man will follow. David recognized the importance of the favor of God for his own life. He wrote, **"For thou, Lord, wilt bless the righteous; with favour wilt thou compass him as with a shield"** (Psalm 5:12). That is powerful. When David stood before the giant, the favor of God shielded him.

When you face the giants in your life, the favor of God will be your shield. His promises are true and the rest is up to you! Improve. Seek to know, understand, and operate in the favor of God.

> When you face the giants in your life,
> the favor of God will be your shield.

Solomon, David's son and the wisest man who ever lived, wrote, **"A good man obtaineth favour of the Lord . . ."** (Proverbs 12:2). David did not need Saul's armor to fight Goliath. He simply needed a shield – *the favor of God.*

Sharpening Your Discernment Skills

Another area of self-improvement comes in sharpening your discernment skills. The Spirit of truth will show and teach you all things (John 16:13).

Saul had made a very generous offer to the one who could take down the giant, but David was not motivated by a desire for money or fame. In everything he did at this time in his life, his purpose was to obey God and then give Him the glory.

What choices do we make when opportunities are offered to us? Only a greedy person says "yes" to everything offered to him. Only a person filled with greed takes things he does not need. A true servant will recognize if an opportunity is better suited for someone else. With a pure heart and right motives, a true servant will share some God-given opportunities with others.

Develop your discernment skills. Discernment is God's sixth sense in you. It is the uncovering of things, allowing one to see beyond the surface of things and then responding in God's wisdom.

Every time God gets ready to elevate you, the devil will come along with a counterfeit opportunity. He will use people who will try to catch some of the opportunity that God has prepared for you. Their attitude is, "If it wasn't for me, you wouldn't have had this opportunity." It is just like the devil to try and steal the glory that is due to God alone.

As you grow in discernment, you will understand when God removes certain people from your life. He may allow partnerships to diminish. He may remove someone close to you. It is painful to experience severed relationships, but as you develop discernment you will recognize God's hand in the matter. Ultimately God will get the glory.

Developing Your Faith

Yes, we must learn to decipher things, but we must also continue to develop our faith in God. He has a plan for you. If your heart is right and you trust in God, then you will have everything you need. You may be trying to figure out how you are going to do what God has told you to do, but when you have improved yourself – learned from the Word and you have disciplined yourself – you can trust God with the rest.

Opportunity does not mean no opposition. Even when opportunity comes, you will still have some giants to face. Just because you have a God-given opportunity doesn't mean you will not have challenges or obstacles. Refuse to allow the devil to turn you around and make you doubt or lose trust. Stand firm. Be steadfast and develop your faith. Contemplate the faithfulness of God. Recount the times He has been faithful to you. Has He ever failed you or anyone you know yet?

> "I will sing of the mercies of the Lord for ever:
> with my mouth will I make known
> thy faithfulness to all generations"
> (Psalm 89:1).

In Second Peter 1:5-7, we find that we can improve our faith by adding to it. It is our choice to improve. Make it a regular practice to add to your faith. According to Peter, you can add goodness, knowledge, self-control, perseverance, godliness, brotherly kindness, and love to your faith. Also, you can possess these qualities in increasing measure. As you add these things to your faith, you will find that they will keep you from being unproductive and ineffective in your call. Wow! The choice is yours. Do you want to be more effective? More productive? Then, choose to improve.

David had no doubt in God's ability to deliver Goliath into his hand. His faith in God was strong.

The Only Way Up Is Down

On your way up, don't forget to go down. The Bible says that David took his staff and went walking. He looked down, stooped down, reached into a stream of water, and grabbed five smooth stones. He chose five smooth stones.

We can improve in our choosing if we go down. "Down" is symbolic of our humility and bowing down to God's authority and direction, bowing down to God in prayer, asking for God's help.

It was no accident that David chose five stones. Remember what the number five means. It means *grace*. David's choice was engineered by God. As we bow down to God, we can ask what we will. The Word says, **"Humble yourselves in the sight of the Lord, and he shall lift you up"** (James 4:10). **"Humble yourselves therefore under the mighty hand of God, that he may exalt you in due time"** (1 Peter 5:6).

David didn't just reach down and guess how many stones he could get off from his slingshot before the giant clobbered him. I believe in David's choice there was divine design. God gave David a witty invention. God gave him something unusual.

"Thou therefore, my son, be strong in the grace
that is in Christ Jesus"
(2 Timothy 2:1).

If you don't mind going down on your knees and seeking God; if you don't mind staying on your face before God; if you don't mind spending days in the desert with God and God alone; if you don't mind going down, then God has great things for you. God wants to remove the things that the world has attached to you. He wants to show you some great and mighty things you know not of (Jeremiah 33:3).

> "Who is this King of glory?
> The Lord strong and mighty,
> the Lord mighty in battle"
> (Psalm 24:8).

Sometimes the things God shows or tells you may seem crazy. How crazy is going up against a nine-foot giant with only five little stones? David had a God-given opportunity, but he had to go down to find his resources. Then he came up with a plan from God. Down in the stream David found grace to do what God had called him to do. God wants lip service, but He also wants face service – on your face in His presence.

Learn to rock until the enemy drops from your life. Rock until his voice and authority are gone from your life. God has given you His grace.

> "Therefore, as ye abound in every thing, in faith,
> and utterance, and knowledge,
> and in all diligence, and in your love to us,
> see that ye abound in this grace also"
> (2 Corinthians 8:7).

In your quest for God's opportunity, you may have faced some giants. Fear has tried to stop you. Friends have tried to misdirect you. Your finances, or lack of, have held you back. But thank God you went down and came up with a rock!

Here is your rock. David said, **"I come to thee in the name of the Lord of hosts . . ."** (1 Samuel 17:45). I can see him in my mind, winding up that rock in the sling.

What devil can stop you? What situation is holding you back? Is there a giant in your pathway? Wind up that slingshot and prepare to release your rock. Release it at your giant and tell that giant that he is coming down.

Friend, the only thing that can hold you back from your divine appointment is you. So improve you! The devil can't stop you. He can't block you. Seize your opportunity.

You may have lost some battles in the past, but this year you have more grace. God has given you another rock. You may have made some bad decisions in the past, but the new improved you is coming up.

Friends may look at you as if you are nuts and fanatical. They may try to tell you that you are not equipped, but you have a rock. On Christ the solid Rock you stand. All other ground is sinking sand. Go to the Rock that is higher!

I am ready to stone the kingdom of darkness. How about you?

By love serve one another.

Galatians 5:13

Chapter 3

Lessons in Servanthood – Preparation for Leadership

It is time to take advantage of God's opportunities coming your way. If you are constantly improving in God and working on yourself from the inside out, it will be evident. Not only will it show, but you will be able to seize the coming opportunities which will literally catapult you into your destiny and purpose.

Opportunity Is Seasonal

Please note that opportunity is seasonal. What God gives to you now or today may never come around again. Since opportunities come in seasons, we must prepare ourselves "in the season" for the season yet to come.

You must understand that whatever position you are in now is merely an opportunity given to you by God to learn and grow and prepare for your next assignment. Stop complaining about your "now." It's not necessary. Whatever pursuit you are in, God is just giving you a little time to get it together, to learn, and to sharpen yourself so you can move into the next season of your life with ease.

The Role of a Shepherd

We see God preparing David to be captain of His army and king of Israel. David, as a shepherd boy, had been anointed for kingship, but there were some qualities he needed to develop to become king. He had to learn to be caring and loving in nature as a shepherd. Otherwise, he would not be suitable to lead as king. In learning to care for the sheep, he would better understand caring for God's people.

A shepherd's duties are far greater than sitting on a rock and watching them eat, sleep, and play nearby. Sheep by nature are not smart. It is sad but true and Scripture likens believers to sheep. Sheep must be led. Without a leader, they wander and get into trouble. They don't know how to avoid briars. They have no coping skills to protect themselves against wild beasts. They are not swift on their feet and they are easily confused. It is the shepherd who guides and protects them.

Sheep do not watch where they are going. They tire easily and when they are thirsty, they don't even know how to find water. A shepherd must locate and lead the sheep to green pastures and still waters.

Sheep are easy prey, not only for beasts of the field, but there are insects that feed on and annoy sheep. A shepherd must know the different types of ointments to apply to the unique sores and infestations that sheep contract. Sheep cannot self-medicate. They cannot protect themselves. The shepherd is required to give comfort and continuous care to the sheep. He must have the quality of stick-to-it-ive-ness.

However, there is one thing sheep do know and that is the most important thing of all. They know the voice of the shepherd, and they know how to follow that voice.

David gave us the outline for a shepherd in the 23rd Psalm. He was a shepherd, but he recognized the ultimate example of shepherding came from the Lord, who was his Shepherd.

Let's look at this Psalm in *The Amplified Bible* as we meditate on the goodness of our Shepherd:

The Lord is my Shepherd [to feed, guide, and shield me]. I shall not lack.

He makes me lie down in [fresh, tender] green pastures; He leads me beside the still and restful waters.

He refreshes and restores my life (my self); He leads me in the paths of righteousness [uprightness and right standing with Him – not for my earning it, but] for His name's sake.

Yes, though I walk through the [deep, sunless] valley of the shadow of death, I will fear or dread no evil, for You are

with me; Your rod [to protect] and Your staff [to guide], they comfort me.

You prepare a table before me in the presence of my enemies. You anoint my head with oil; my [brimming] cup runs over.

Surely or only goodness, mercy, and unfailing love shall follow me all the days of my life, and through the length of my days the house of the Lord [and His presence] shall be my dwelling place.

Psalm 23:1-6 AMP

It is the duty of a shepherd to keep the sheep from want or need. He must be one who exercises authority with wisdom. That's what Psalm 23 says. He makes them lie down. The waters he leads them to refresh and restore their soul. In other words, a shepherd helps to bring new life. If the shepherd did not do these things, the sheep would wander in frenzy and soon lose their lives.

The Leading of the Good Shepherd

The Good Shepherd leads His sheep into paths of righteousness. He leads them in the way they should go, for His name's sake, so God will receive the glory. Even when we as His sheep walk near the valley of death, the Good Shepherd is with us. Sheep have no fear when a good shepherd is near.

> Sheep have no fear when a
> good shepherd is near.

David learned in the field to be a good shepherd, which gave him great qualities to be a good leader.

A good shepherd uses his rod and his staff not to beat or flog the sheep, but to gently guide them in the way that they should go. Even though evil may lurk about, a good shepherd sees to it that his sheep are fed. He anoints their head with oil. It is an oil of protection, to keep insects from infecting the sheep and thereby causing discomfort or death to the animal.

> By His Word and His Spirit,.
> God leads us in the way we should go.

Our Good Shepherd anoints us with the oil of the sweet Holy Spirit for our comfort and consolation. Because of His leadership, goodness and mercy follow us and we have the promise of dwelling with Him forever.

> "Goodness and mercy shall follow me all the days of my life, and I will dwell in the house of the Lord for ever" (Psalm 23:6).

There is no better example of what a true shepherd should be than this. A shepherd is concerned with the flock and yet will go and search for the one lost sheep that has wandered away.

David learned the way of a shepherd and he served his sheep as their master. As he served the sheep, he honored his Great Shepherd in the field, worshiping and having fellowship with Him.

Diligent Through Discipline

David had developed the quality of serving diligently. Many times we start out doing well, but then we get tired or unfocused. This is an area we must improve in. We must learn to be diligent through discipline.

David was often called upon to go and play the harp for King Saul to ease his nerves. Saul was troubled by demons and when David played the harp, the anointed music would drive the demons from Saul's mind. David responded whenever Saul needed him. It was part of David's nature as a servant.

Most of us would respond differently to an opportunity to play for the king. We would hire a publicist and get an interview with *People* magazine so everyone would know that we were great and that we played for the king. We would start a concert tour, cut an album, and the sheep would be a thing of the past that we never mention again.

But not David. He was a true shepherd. When he finished his moment of ministry, he went right back to his flock. **"And whatsoever ye do in word or** deed, do all in the name of the Lord Jesus, giving thanks to God and the Father by him" (Colossians 3:17). God still had things to teach David about servanthood and David responded to discipline. David was not playing games in the field. He was learning from God, having fellowship with Him, and growing in Him. David's future depended on it.

Understand, both the shepherd and the king need a warrior spirit because there are lions and bears, demons and devils, in both duties. David had to withstand pestilence and bad weather, discomfort, and disease with his sheep. These things he would have to deal with as king. What is God preparing you for?

We must learn how to smile in all circumstances. The clouds come and difficulties arise for everyone, but as a shepherd and a servant, a good leader will keep his eyes on God. He will not look at the clouds or see only the difficulties. He will be focused on the Deliverer. There is a process we go through before we go to our next place in God.

Destiny Is Progressive

Destiny is progressive. You do not jump into it. Destiny has levels. God moves us from level to level, from glory to glory, ever higher as we grow in Him.

"My times are in thy [God's] hand . . ." (Psalm 31:15). "For my thoughts are not your thoughts, neither are your ways my ways, saith the Lord" (Isaiah 55:8). As a servant, I must remind myself that God is in charge. I don't like to

67

face difficulties, but there is no other way to grow. If David had never faced a lion or a bear, he would have never had the courage to face a giant. He may have had the opportunity, but not the courage.

Many of us want to do great things for God, but we don't want to face difficulties that come with growth. We must learn to conquer our fears by facing our lions and bears. We must learn to recognize that at every new level in God there will be a new devil, a new circumstance to persevere through and to obtain victory over.

> "Be strong and of a good courage; be not afraid, neither be thou dismayed: for the Lord thy God is with thee whithersoever thou goest"
> (Joshua 1:9).

So What's Your Giant?

Your lions and bears are the private battles you wage that no one knows about but you. That is why you are in that field. It is just you and God, and your secret is safe with Him. As you grow in Him and learn of Him, He will impart wisdom and strength to help you overcome.

It is critical that God work out the insecurities, fears, pride, or anything else that might defeat you as you pursue your purpose. We have all heard the saying, Solomon recognized that pride alone could take someone down (Proverbs 16:18). Pride alone can lead you straight into destruction.

> "Pride goeth before destruction,
> and an haughty spirit before a fall"
> (Proverbs 16:18).

Some have lions of nicotine. You can't face your giant if a cigarette still has a hold on you. As soon as you get ready to fight, you could get a coughing fit, your blood pressure could shoot up, or you could have a heart attack right where you stand.

You have to kill that thing. Whatever deadly thing threatens your destiny in God must be put to death. Kill it before it destroys you. Low self-esteem, bad temper, substance abuse, addictions, pride, a controlling spirit, a lying spirit, a poverty mentality, judgmentalism, or a lack of self-control. These things kill and killing is the devil's business, along with stealing and destroying. We want no part of that.

Kill the lack of discipline, the laziness, that pride, and low self-esteem. Search the Scriptures to find what God has to say on the matter and hit the devil with the Word of God. Hit him hard. Make him hurt. You have an opportunity waiting.

Building Your Resistance to the Enemy

I know how to fight the devil, because we had a showdown. He said that he was going to kill me and

I told him that he was going to be the one to die. You see, I have been fighting. I have had to develop personal and inner strength.

> "Behold, I give unto you power to tread
> on serpents and scorpions,
> and over all the power of the enemy:
> and nothing shall by any means hurt you"
> (Luke 10:19).

My husband, as great as he is, cannot develop strength for me. I had to get my own muscles. I had to get something down on the inside, and I couldn't send anyone to the gym in my place. All they would do is get my muscles. They won't be able to bring them home and put them on me!

Have you been to the gym lately? Have you had any resistance lately? You must resist the devil and he will flee from you (James 4:7). You must develop muscles and strength to defeat the weaknesses in your life. The Goliath of opportunity is coming. Will you be strong enough to take him down? Yes, you will if you kill your lions and your bears first!

> "Submit yourselves therefore to God.
> Resist the devil,
> and he will flee from you"
> (James 4:7).

Building Your Confidence in God

Part of David's preparation for greatness was gaining confidence. He did not get a big head or all pumped up about himself. He learned through his time with God who he was in Him. It is not about a position – yours or anyone's. It is about who called you and what He has called you to be. If you get a big head about your call, you might be a little embarrassed, particularly if you have not clearly heard from God.

David was not about bragging. He didn't walk onto the battlefield acting as if he was God's gift to the army, even though he was! He was full of confidence in God, not full of himself. He was so confident that he did not give a moment of thought to the circumstances. He didn't consider the money or the maiden. He was there as a servant of the Most High God.

> David was full of confidence in God, not full of himself.

As you face your challenges you will grow. You will increase in strength. You will increase in wisdom. You will increase in faith. This kind of strength is not about muscles. It's all about who you are in God. As you overcome each new challenge, your confidence will increase.

You see, you are God's child. You are God's answer to someone's mess, hurt, or heartache. You are a watchman on the wall. You are a guardian of His sheep. You are His servant. Have you taken responsibility for whose you are? Are you prepared? Have you been preparing? Have you spent time with God? Is your life spent in fellowship and worship of Him?

Do you know that the Lord is on your side? David knew that the Lord had delivered the lion and the bear into his hands. He knew, without a doubt, that with the help of the Lord, he would take down that giant.

Waiting Upon the Lord

If it had not been for the Lord on my side, I may have lost my mind. I could have lost my business. Maybe I would have been on drugs or in an insane asylum. But, the Lord fought my battles. I waited on the Lord and He renewed my strength (Isaiah 40:31). I learned to fly and to run and not become weary while facing His opportunities.

God has been pushing me. I have been in the workout room of my faith and God has been challenging me to do more to build more strength. To fine-tune my hearing. To be strengthened in my inner man/woman (Ephesians 3:16). Is God pushing you? Will you obey and get prepared for your next assignment? Again, I exhort you, if you want to be a leader, learn to serve.

> If you want to be a leader, learn to serve.

God Is Calling You!

Do you feel that destiny is calling on you? God is calling you to move closer, because your opportunity is near. Remember the Boy Scout motto: "Be prepared." Remember the words of Bishop T. D. Jakes: "Get ready! Get ready! Get ready! Get ready! Get ready! Get ready!"

Remember the words of Jeremiah: **"For I know the thoughts that I think toward you, saith the Lord, thoughts of peace, and not of evil, to give you an expected end"** (Jeremiah 29:11). Remember the words of Jesus, **"Go ye"** (Matthew 28:19; Mark 16:15). He is calling you!

Do not allow another day to pass you by. **"Study to shew thyself approved unto God, a workman that needeth not to be ashamed, rightly dividing the word of truth"** (2 Timothy 2:15).

God is calling you! Learn from God's Word. Develop your faith and commit yourself to servanthood. Lift up the name of Jesus, because when He is lifted up, He will draw all men unto Himself (John 12:32), and you will discover new heights in Him. This is your hour! This is your moment of grace!

"Grace be to you and peace from God our Father,
and from the Lord Jesus Christ"
(2 Corinthians 1:2).

For who are you, O great mountain [of human obstacles]? Before Zerubbabel [who with Joshua had led the return of the exiles from Babylon and was undertaking the rebuilding of the temple, before him] you shall become a plain [a mere molehill]! And he shall bring forth the finishing gable stone [of the new temple] with loud shoutings of the people, crying, Grace, grace to it!

Zechariah 4:7 AMP

Chapter 4

A Greater Portion of Grace

In studying the life of David, I began to vividly understand and greatly appreciate the gift of God's grace. The anointing of God came when David was yet a boy. It was not only an anointing of God, but it was also a manifestation of the grace of God that was given David for his assignment and purpose.

The anointing came to the house of Jesse, but it was not for him. It was not for his other sons. It was for David for an assignment from God.

As I studied I felt as if David was literally speaking to me from the sands of time. I was hungry to know about God's grace on David's life, and I began to listen to hear what the Spirit would say through David.

Seize Opportunity — It's YOUR Season!

Grace Brings New Horizons

David was an early riser, so he started on me in the wee hours of the morning in my bedroom. Morning is symbolic of new opportunity. God's mercies and His grace are new every morning.

It is of the Lord's mercies that we are not consumed, because his compassions fail not.

They are new every morning: great is thy faithfulness.

Lamentations 3:22-23

If you think you can only hear from God in church, you can learn something here. Each new day brings a new or an additional assignment. It was on the eve before David's father gave the instructions to go to the battlefield to carry food to his brothers, but it was the next morning when David moved on the assignment. We cannot let nighttime cancel our assignment. In the midst of the darkness God said, **"Let there be light . . ."** (Genesis 1:3).

"David rose up early in the morning . . ." (1 Samuel 17:20). In observation, David was saying that grace causes new horizons. The grace of God will not lead you where His grace cannot keep you. David did not decide when it was time to leave the field. His father did. I am sure that someone was appointed to take David's place and care for the sheep, and knowing human nature, I am sure there was some lack of understanding in the household. I'm sure the sheep-keeper wondered, *Where is David*

78

going? Why is he leaving the sheep with me? Is he coming back?

> The grace of God will not lead you where His grace cannot keep you.

You may not understand why things are changing in your church, in the leadership, in the lives of someone you love, or in the circumstances of your own life. You do not need to understand, but you do need to obey the Father because when the winds of change come, grace is forcing you onto a new horizon, into a different atmosphere, a strange climate. That same grace is sufficient to keep you.

Grace Is the Overseer of Purpose

David could have accomplished nothing without the grace of God. Outside of grace we can do nothing in and of ourselves. I realize grace is only given for the assignment or circumstance at hand. Grace is the overseer of purpose. It helps you bring it to pass. You don't get a bucket full to store up. God gives more grace as the burdens and labors grow greater (Ephesians 4:7). We are administrators or stewards (servants) of His manifold grace in the earth (1 Peter 4:10).

> "But by the grace of God I am what I am:
> and his grace which was bestowed upon me
> was not in vain; but I laboured more abundantly
> than they all: yet not I,
> but the grace of God which was with me"
> (1 Corinthians 15:10).

To understand grace more fully, perhaps you should take a look back on your life. You could probably write a book about the many times God's grace was there for you. When you were sick and almost died, His grace was sufficient – the exact portion you needed. When you faced bankruptcy, His grace was sufficient. When your kid messed up and was facing jail, God's grace was sufficient. When you had that abortion, God's grace was there. When you were talked about and lied on, grace had your back covered.

> "Grace be unto you, and peace, from him which is,
> and which was, and which is to come . . ."
> (Revelation 1:4).

It is true what the old-timers used to say: "Truly, God has brought me from a mighty long way." Well, God is still bringing you out today. His grace is covering you and converting you into a person of excellence.

You Are Being Set Up!

Perhaps you have achieved scholastically. Maybe you have received a better position at your job, or you have learned a new trade. You are in a wholesome, God-given relationship. You are living holy and you are in the Word of God daily. You have a new hope. You have been faithful in the field, but still something is up.

God's grace is calling you to come up higher. He is getting ready to set you up. Royal blood flows through your veins, so no matter the past, God's grace is flowing your way and He is moving you into your kingship – your opportunity is at hand.

Your ways are not God's ways (Isaiah 55:8), so you can be sure that there are no tried and true formulas that you will be able to fall back on. This new thing is a walk of faith. Faith that you developed in the field. The Word tells us that we are to **"walk by faith, not by sight"** (2 Corinthians 5:7).

> "We having the same spirit of faith, according as it is written, I believed, and therefore have I spoken; we also believe, and therefore speak" (2 Corinthians 4:13).

In the field, you knew what to expect. You may have gotten comfortable in the field. In the field you had a grip. You knew your limits. You knew what equipment you needed and you knew how to do your job better than anyone.

In this year of grace, I believe that everyone who has been faithful in the field is going to receive a new assignment – a bigger opportunity. If you have been prepared, God has already put it in your spirit. It is churning around in your belly. You may not have the full revelation of how it will come to pass, but then there will be manifold grace.

So it was with David. He probably sensed something. That's why he gave sheep to a sheep-keeper and food to a food-keeper, but it was not until he went up to the battlefield that opportunity met him.

> "The Lord shall increase you more and more,
> you and your children"
> (Psalm 115:14).

Fear Not!

Fear not! Every opportunity is to take us to another level in God, not to knock us down. Transition is always upward. God wants to take us from glory to glory. In David's opportune moment, he did not know how he was going to kill Goliath, but he spoke in faith: **"The Lord that delivered**

82

me out of the paw of the lion, and out of the paw of the bear, he will deliver me out of the hand of this Philistine . . ." (1 Samuel 17:37). David had complete confidence that his Deliverer would come.

When you have been through something and God has delivered you, you develop confidence, not just in your ability but in God's ability which supersedes yours. You can boldly confess that surely God will deliver you from the next big giant that you face. Right?

You need to get that confidence deep down in your belly. Oral Roberts calls that place "your knower." You will know, in your knower, that God's grace will deliver you.

> "Nay, in all these things we are more than conquerors through him that loved us"
> (Romans 8:37).

"Opportunity is in your vicinity!"

Hear the words of God's prophet: "Opportunity is in your vicinity!" You may have felt as though you have been in some cosmic holding pattern in your life. It may seem to you that you are between seasons. It may seem like an eternity since you have had any sense of movement, but you are faithful in the field. When you are faithful, you are full of faith. Simple, isn't it?

Faithfulness is a character trait of your Father. You must be growing to be more and more like Him. Yes, God is a faithful God. He is a rewarder of those who diligently seek Him (Hebrews 11:6). He has not forgotten you out there on that hillside with your little responsibilities. All He has required of you is faithfulness until He makes a change. Your change will come.

Understand, we cannot make our change happen. Oh, we can, but when we do, we make a mess of things. In case you are in dobut, go back to the Word and read about the Ishmael mess that Abram and Sarai made (Genesis 16). Trying to make God's Word come to pass in your flesh can have monumental repercussions. That one did and it is still playing out in our news each day. **"Be still, and know that I am God . . ."** (Psalm 46:10).

Do not fret. Someone or something will come and get you out of that field. The Father came and got David. He will come to get you too. Be faithful where you are and you will be faithful where you are going.

> "Be still, and know that I am God . . ."
> (Psalm 46:10).

Moving Up Higher

One morning while I was getting my hair done — fried, dyed, and laid to the side — I was taking care of several business matters. I was talking to people on the phone, making decisions about renovations, planning a luncheon, and so forth. My hair stylist said to me, "I didn't know you do all those things." I replied, "Honey, I do whatever I have to do till my new season comes." Whatever God requires of me, I am His. I am coming and going.

The Bible says David came and went from Saul's quarters to the father's fields, from playing the harp to tending the sheep. When it was time, the father came and got him. He left the field. When it is time, God will call me by name, "Come here, little one. Come up higher!"

> "Come here, little one. Come up higher!"

David was the baby boy, unskilled and inexperienced in royalty. However, he was pronounced king. Perhaps you are the least likely to achieve anything according to your high school yearbook. Maybe you are the youngest. The poorest. You are the one who did not graduate. You may feel you have messed up so badly that God would never use you.

Here's good news for you! **"God hath chosen the foolish things of the world to confound the wise; and God hath chosen the weak things of the world to confound the things which are mighty"** (1 Corinthians 1:27).

God can make something out of nothing. He can make a way out of no way. He knew all about you before you were even born (Psalm 139:15-16). Your mistakes didn't take Him by surprise. He has not thrown you out on some garbage heap. He made provision for your mess through the precious blood of His Son, Jesus.

In another unusual circumstance of David's life, he was called upon to go to King Saul and play the harp for him. David was serving the very man he had been anointed to replace. Perhaps you have cried because someone else got the position you felt was meant for you. Keep serving God. It may be a setup for them to get up and get out. You sought the Lord. He understood your cry (2 Samuel 22:7). He has manifold grace for you. Before that king knew it, his anointing was transferred and harp boy was wearing the crown!

> "Grace be unto you, and peace,
> from God our Father, and from the Lord Jesus Christ.
> I thank my God always on your behalf,
> for the grace of God which is
> given you by Christ Jesus"
> (1 Corinthians 1:3-4).

Grace Will Provide Your Platform

You may face some challenges, but God specializes in the unusual, the invincible, the incomparable, the insurmountable. You may not see it yet, because it is happening in the supernatural. Get ready though because grace is upon you. Grace is pushing you. Grace is keeping you. Grace provides a platform to stand on for the unusual.

It's your time. It's your opportunity. You already have the burden for it. When David reached the battlefield, he had an immediate burden for the army of the Lord. You have the anointing for it. You don't have everything you need to do the task yet, but you will have the grace to accomplish it.

> "Wherefore gird up the loins of your mind,
> be sober, and hope to the end for the grace that is to be
> brought unto you at the revelation of Jesus Christ"
> (1 Peter 1:13).

I understand what it feels like to carry the burden for your purpose. The call sometimes seems heavy. You may beg for your turn some days and other days you cower in fear at the enormity of it all. Even though you realize you do not have what you need to fulfill your call, you cannot shake it. When God's grace comes on you for the task, it will produce supernatural faith.

Supernatural Faith

The next thing that God is calling us to as the Body of Christ and as individuals will not be accomplished with our basic level of faith. This thing is bigger than anything we have faced in the past. It will cost more than we have. We may not have the right people in place to help us with it, but God's grace will cover it all. We will have everything we need in the Holy Ghost.

It is time to walk in supernatural faith. You may think you are talking crazy, but when you are under the anointing it is just your faith talking. As you self-improve in your faith, you will begin to say, "I can do all things through Christ who strengthens me. I can buy my new home, and I can start my business. I can develop my ministry."

> "I can do all things through Christ
> which strengtheneth me"
> (Philippians 4:13).

David's own brothers thought he was crazy, but he had supernatural faith. Faith was so strong in David, a lad was able to convince a king!

When we, as men and women of God, begin to speak in supernatural faith, believing what we are saying, then we are going to go higher.

> "He [Abraham] staggered not
> at the promise of God through unbelief;
> but was strong in faith, giving glory to God.
> And being fully persuaded, that what he had promised,
> he was able also to perform"
> (Romans 4:20-21).

Supernatural power hit that rock. A rock alone could do nothing more to Goliath than give him a headache. When God adds His power to what is in your hand, look out. That rock had supernatural trajectory. I imagine it broke the sound barrier long before it was known that we had one!

The Anointed Rock!

When you seize your opportunity, you are going to need something. You may think, *Yeah, I'll need money. I'll need a staff. I'll need real estate. I'll need influence.* But I tell you this, I say, "God, give me a rock, one that has been anointed by You!"

Years ago Dottie Rambo wrote a wonderful song, "I Go to the Rock." God is our rock, our fortress, and our salvation (Psalm 91:2). He is our "anointed rock" dealer. One anointed rock will destroy the enemies of God. I was empty handed until God gave me some rocks!

I used to wonder why David chose five stones when one filled the need. I felt the Holy Ghost answer rise up in my spirit, saying, "David only needed one rock to destroy the enemy. One rock was grace and the four remaining were more grace." That is manifold grace.

> "Grace and peace be multiplied unto you through the knowledge of God, and of Jesus our Lord"
> (2 Peter 1:2).

I am killing a big demon today and I have a little something – something for the next devil. Satan, I'll take you down with one rock, but when you come at me again, I have four more where that one came from. I have grace and more grace. I have manifold grace. **"I can do all things through Christ which strengtheneth me"** (Philippians 4:13).

Is something trying to stop you from God's purpose and destiny? Pick up a rock. If the enemy is messing with your mind, show him The Rock. Goliath had a sword and a shield, but David had a rock – The Rock of Ages!

What is keeping you from your purpose and destiny? Seize your opportunity. Grab hold of The Rock. Ready, set, throw! It's your season!

Product Information

Signs of a Committed Christian
Seize Opportunity - Book
Not Yet, Not Ever Count Me Out
Morning Coffee (Coffee I Don't Like Your
Church (Series)
(scented candle) $6.00
Enslaved
Stretch Forth Your Hand
Seize Opportunity (Series)
While in Babylon
God Has Great Plans for You!
He's Ready When You Are
What A Word Is This?
PaPa Abraham (Series)
Word Has Power
A Special Love
After the Resurrection (Series)
The Cleansing is Over But I? am Not Finish
The Attitude of a Remnant
The Glory (Series)
Rich Man Poor Man
Self Improvement

Products available in: **Audio $5.00 VHS $12.00
CD $10.00 DVD $20.00**

Credit Cards accepted: *American Express,*
MasterCard, *Visa*, **and** *Discover*.

Information needed:

Name:_____

Address_____

City, State, Zip_____

Phone _____

Item	Type	Qty	Cost

Credit Card number and expiration date

_____Exp._____

Check (please include drivers license number)

_____

Contact Information

Debra Morton Ministries
P.O. Box 871265
New Orleans, LA 70187
(504) 244-6800
Ext. 3051 or 3017